IN OLD PHOTOGRAPHS

BRITAIN

HORSHAM

PAST & PRESENT

DAVID ARSCOTT

SUTTON PUBLISHING

Sutton Publishing Limited
Phoenix Mill · Thrupp · Stroud
Gloucestershire · GL5 2BU

First published 2002

Copyright © David Arscott, 2002

Title page: The Causeway in 1905, when the road
was still unmetalled. *John Cannon*

British Library Cataloguing in Publication Data
A catalogue record for this book is available from the
British Library.

ISBN 0-7509-2780-1

Typeset in 10.5/13.5 Photina.
Typesetting and origination by
Sutton Publishing Limited.
Printed and bound in England by
J.H. Haynes & Co. Ltd, Sparkford.

The very last day of the market in Bishopric, 1913. *John Cannon*

CONTENTS

Middle Street, 1913. Traffic was, of course, much lighter then, but the street was originally a two-way thoroughfare and the policeman had a vital role to play. *John Cannon*

INTRODUCTION

Horsham can be perplexing. The first-time visitor arriving by car is swept into the snarling canyon of Albion Way, funnelled deftly into a multi-storey car park and deposited in a teeming shopping mall whose exits lead to a warren of bustling narrow streets and twittens. The recent incomer who has learned to negotiate these interconnecting, often pedestrianised, thoroughfares will nevertheless experience difficulty in relating their abrupt twists and turns to the geography of a town which has occupied the site for more than a thousand years. So much has changed – and so recently.

One might expect long-term residents to be most dismayed by the transformations of the past thirty years, but this proves not to be the case. There are, of course, grumbles about certain well-loved features gone for ever and less than sensitive buildings erected in their place, but this is a major restructuring of urban space which has passed the ultimate test: the locals like it. True, the demands of the internal combustion engine have been recognised and sometimes brutally accommodated, but large areas of the centre of town have been miraculously reclaimed for those who would rather stand and stare and shop.

The past, meanwhile, remains all about us. The network of streets around Carfax is still recognisably that first laid down many centuries ago, and 'house detectives' clambering into tight loft spaces have discovered numerous traces of medieval buildings hidden behind more recent façades. The town has constantly renewed itself, the glass-lined passageways of modern Swan Walk being both an echo and a continuation of an arrangement which countless generations have found to their taste.

Old cottages in North Street, near the junction with Park Street, *c.* 1905. There are few ancient survivors among the modern developments here – and a long section of the street has disappeared altogether. *John Cannon*

West Street, *c.* 1905. This major shopping street is now pedestrianised. *Cecil Cramp*

Horsham's founding fathers were Saxon colonisers of the Sussex Weald, an area notorious for its sticky clay and dense covering of sturdy oaks and beeches. Farmers preferred to plough the fertile fields of the coastal plain and the downland slopes, but they drove their animals upcountry during the spring and summer months to find fresh pasturage. These seasonal journeys created a system of north–south greenways, and settlements developed at favourable sites along the way. Place names are a rich source of fanciful speculation, but Horsham's does indeed appear to derive from an association with horses. Breeders and trainers found the spot congenial, because it was at a convenient crossing of the River Arun and close to tracts of well-drained greensand countryside in St Leonard's Forest where their stock could be moved in winter. Their growing community must swiftly have attracted people with complementary skills, until the place became a permanent and flourishing trading centre.

After the Norman conquest of 1066 Sussex was divided into five (later six) administrative 'rapes', each running north-south with a port, a major castle close by and a chain of lesser castles extending into the Weald. Horsham, rapidly developing into one of the largest towns in the rape of Bramber, lay within easy reach of the minor fortifications at Chennelsbrook, Sedgwick and Knepp. By about 1140 it had a substantial church (which would be rebuilt in the Early English style in about 1250) and early in the thirteenth century it was given borough status and an annual fair. In 1295 the local 'burgesses' were summoned to send two representatives to the King's parliament at Westminster, while the assizes first came here in 1307 and a county court sitting is recorded in 1316 – by which time many impressive houses had been built and the first permanent retail premises had been established. Horsham had undoubtedly arrived.

During the sixteenth and seventeenth centuries the Weald was home to a clangorous and highly profitable iron industry which supplied armaments to the government and ploughs to farmers. Horsham, sharing this prosperity, later became a staging post for the coaching trade and the fulcrum of a range of rural industries, including brickmaking, tanning and brewing. The county gaol was transferred here from Lewes in the 1530s and was to stay – at various sites – for more than 300 years. The town became a military headquarters during the Napoleonic Wars (a barracks was built on the southern outskirts) and was given a further boost by the coming of the railway in the 1840s. By the time that the older photographs in this book were taken, Horsham had all the accoutrements of a comfortable market town, with its substantial public buildings, small factories and crowded, well-stocked shops.

The town's fortunes have certainly sometimes wavered during the intervening period – the late twentieth century remodelling of the centre was a last-ditch attempt to prevent its decline into a virtual satellite of neighbouring Crawley – but modern industries such as electronics, pharmaceuticals and insurance have replaced former trades which had reached their allotted span, and by 1990 Horsham had earned the unofficial title of 'top boom town of Britain'. It is doubtful that the place has ever been more prosperous at any time in its history, or (to generalise) that its inhabitants have ever been more content with their lot.

This is unashamedly a book about the centre of the town, where continuities and disruptions make for a fascinating tour. We begin, inevitably, at Carfax, which has for centuries been the hub around which the bustling social and commercial life of Horsham has revolved. Next we visit Middle Street and the town hall before travelling along the Causeway (very little changed) to the church, Normandy and the river. Back in the shopping district, we explore in turn West Street, Bishopric, North Street and East Street (venturing beyond the railway bridge into Queen Street and Brighton Road) before exploring the Springfield Road/London Road area and, finally, venturing a short way along Worthing Road to the south.

Part of the pleasure of picking a way through these criss-crossing highways and byways is to come across a remembered building from a different angle, so that we eventually find ourselves thoroughly familiarised. To tackle the complete itinerary in a single day would be a tiring exercise, perhaps, but nowhere are we more than half a mile from Carfax, and in this small span we find the restless history of the town unfolding before us.

Horsham has been lucky both in its modern historians and in its avid collectors of old photographs and picture postcards. The generosity of the latter (see page 128) has made my task entirely pleasurable and has ensured a wealth of illustrations from which to choose. My own photographs, taken in April 2002, are certainly not intended as collectors' items, but I hope they at least help explain some elements of the streetscape which would otherwise be inscrutable.

Will another such book be required a generation from now? I rather hope not. No community can, or should, resist sensible change, but Horsham is just emerging in surprisingly good heart from a truly cataclysmic upheaval and has surely earned the right to puts its proverbial feet up. A major reconstruction still awaits the Black Horse Way area, creating a Millennium Square with a large department store and new housing. After that, may we please enjoy this engaging West Sussex town as it is for a while?

David Arscott
October 2002

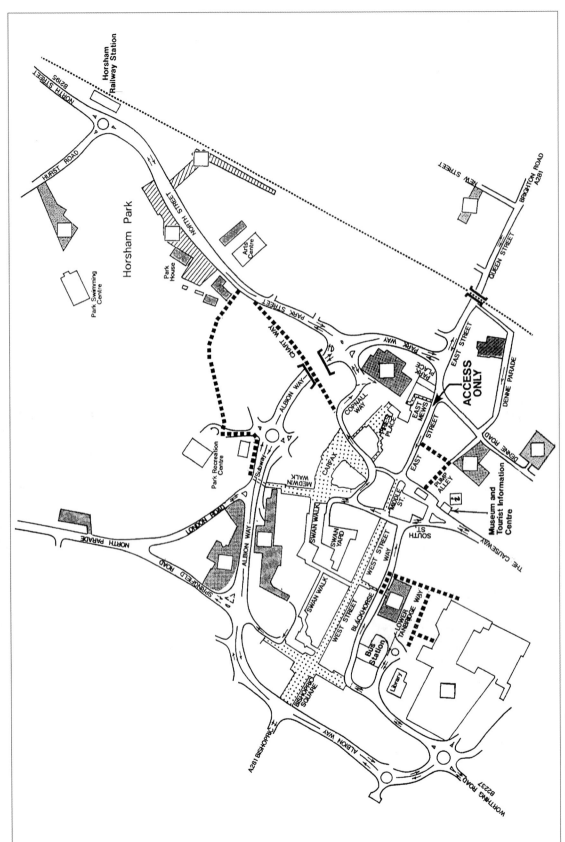

A map of modern Horsham.

1
Carfax

Looking into Carfax from the town hall, *c.* 1908. The approximate date is confirmed by the size of the tree, which was planted in 1891. The name of the town's large central square was formerly Scarfolkes, its meaning unknown. *John Cannon*

The west side of Carfax has seen the greatest changes. In this photograph, taken in about 1906, the Wesleyan Sunday school parades past Lintott's wholesale grocery and provision works. Further to the right, with the semi-circular façade, were the offices of the *West Sussex Gazette*, in a building which later became the Workers' Education Association Hall and, later still, the Women's Institute Market Hall. *Cecil Cramp*

Here we have a good view of Lintott's tall chimney through the arch. Another part of the company's enterprise was candle making. In the foreground, behind railings, are the village stocks. *Cecil Cramp*

The buildings of Swan Walk now stand behind the route of the parade in the photograph on the facing page, while the Sterling Buildings (bottom picture) occupy the Lintott's site: the imposing, pedimented houses which once fronted Carfax were demolished in the late 1930s.

Now we swing round to the north side of Carfax, in a photograph of about 1922 which shows the stocks and whipping post more clearly than on page 10. Behind, with the arch, were the offices of King & Barnes brewery, while the post office (demolished in 1972) occupied the ivy-clad building to the right. *John Cannon*

Today only the house on the left remains. The stocks have been relocated, and there are substantial new blocks on the right of the picture. The post office has moved just a short hop to the site of the old brewery building.

Public transport old and new. The single-decker no. 33 Aldershot & District bus in July 1961 (on its way to Guildford) is on a stretch of road pedestrianised today. *Aldershot & District Bus Interest Group*

Traffic is still allowed in parts of Carfax, although the modern double-decker no. 93 faces in the other direction on its way out of town towards Dorking.

Looking north from Carfax. In the top picture we again see the tree as a fairly young specimen (see page 9), indicating that the view was taken early in the twentieth century. The bandstand can be seen behind it, and the Jubilee fountain in the foreground. The lower photograph dates from about 1930, an addition being the memorial to the fallen of the First World War. The street is already much busier, with several cars and motorbikes on the right of the picture and a bus turning in at the far left. *John Cannon*

Today's view reveals a good deal of continuity, although some of the street 'furniture' (including the fountain and the war memorial) has been moved. Traffic is allowed through this part of Carfax, but the road surface is a deterrent to would-be speed merchants.

The greatest change is apparent only as you approach St Mark's church – which, along with the lower part of North Street, is no longer there. The redundant building was pulled down in 1989 as part of the town centre redevelopment scheme, but a public outcry saved the tower and its spire.

The fountain was in too central a position for modern car and pedestrian management, but it was clearly a proud moment when it was opened in 1897 to mark the sixty years of Queen Victoria's reign. All the local worthies present are listed on the back of the card, along with details of their trade or profession – among them banker, photographer, bookbinder, ironmonger, auctioneer, miller, corn merchant, surgeon and jam maker. On the far left is Jury Cramp who ran a jewellery shop in the town centre and a short-lived temperance hotel (page 36) by the town hall. *Above: John Cannon*

There's a good deal of architectural continuity on the east side of Carfax. The Theatre Royal began life as a cinema, and we shall meet it again on the next page. *Above: John Cannon*

The Electric Theatre opened in 1911, and it was originally approached via the narrow twitten running beside the Stout House. The early photograph was taken in about 1916. In the following year the owners bought the shop to the left of the pub, so giving themselves an impressive new entrance, and they changed the name to the Carfax Theatre. After the Second World War drama began to take prominence over film shows.
Above: Cecil Cramp

Carfax was traditionally the place to gather for major events in Horsham, and here we see large crowds enjoying the sunshine and what seems to be some kind of agricultural event. A careful look through a magnifying glass reveals (I think) just one head without a hat on. The narrow entrance to Piries Place can be seen to the right of the nearest building. *Cecil Cramp*

Today it is clearly named, advertising the shopping precinct seen overleaf.

The central market in Piries Place, 1951. *John Cannon*

Today this is the site of a gleaming iron and glass shopping precinct, with not a headscarf in sight.

Trendy as the precinct may be, the narrow
route back to Carfax leads between a jostle of
older buildings.

The eastern side of Carfax, looking north. The older photograph was taken in about 1960, with the car already king – indeed, more so than today as far as this spot is concerned. *Above: John Cannon*

In 1877 the Duke of Norfolk referred to the large central area of Carfax as 'all that waste and unenclosed land', and the top photograph (looking south) shows that things weren't very different at the beginning of the twentieth century. *Cecil Cramp*

Today's scene certainly looks more lived-in.

The Crown Inn (seen on the right of the pictures on the previous page) shows little change since the top photograph was taken in 1906, although the present tasteful lanterns can't compare with the magnificent lamp standard which stood here a century ago – Horsham had many fine examples then. *John Cannon*

Today's topical touch is a board outside advertising a quiz night.

Resurfacing Carfax in 1948. The Crown Inn can be seen on the left, with the Sterling Buildings behind. Carter & Son on the corner sold shoes. A school of motoring advertises its services above the shop. *Alan Partridge*

Today the tarmac has gone and the street is paved with setts – accessible to motor vehicles, but reminding drivers that the area is to be shared.

The south end of Carfax, 1951. The Glayshers' shop, medieval in origin, was dismantled and taken to the open air museum at Singleton, near Chichester, for re-erection. *John Cannon*

It has been replaced by perhaps the ugliest small building in all Horsham (although see page 32).

King's Head Hotel, Carfax. The top photograph, dated 1907, shows a German prince with the first military Rolls-Royces. The Inland Revenue had its offices here from 1855 until 1881. *John Cannon*

One would hardly think this a matter of pride, but the sign has remained to this day.

Colletts Alley runs between Carfax and Middle
Street, and is commonly known as 'Fish and Chip
alley' because of the popular shop half way along.
Little has changed over recent years save for the
use of the corner premises and the appearance of
a sign forbidding parking at any time. Who would
even try? *Above: John Cannon*

2
Middle Street
& Market Square

Middle Street from the junction with Carfax, *c.* 1935. Originally (page 4) traffic was allowed in both directions, but common sense has by now prevailed. The Tanner & Chart department store can be seen on the left of the picture. Mr Camplin the chemist, opposite, had his own dark room for developing and printing films. *John Cannon*

Middle Street from West Street. The Punch Bowl pub
has gone, but there is surprising continuity between the
photographs taken in 1904 and 2002. An important
change has been the banning of traffic from this narrow
little street. *Above: John Cannon*

Middle Street, at the junction with South Street. Anyone wondering why the Abbey National offices should have a hoist on the top floor will understand once they look at the photograph from the 1920s. Churchman took in its goods at both first- and second-floor level, while the owner and his family lived above the premises in the house on the left. *Above: John Cannon*

The Glaysher family not only had a hardware business in Carfax (page 26) but a similar shop in Middle Street. At the time this photograph was taken, *c.* 1908, Tom Glaysher (third from left under the 'Tools & Hardware' sign) had recently bought the watchmakers and jewellers next door. His assistant, Mr Norris, stands in the doorway on the right. *John Cannon*

Alas, this is another horrible redevelopment job – for which, of course, the Non-Stop Party Shop is itself blameless. The anonymous passer-by on the left has a remarkable resemblance to Mr Glaysher but is presumably not related.

Middle Street, at the junction with Carfax. In 1951 both Camplins the chemist and Chart & Lawrence had survived (see the 1935 photograph on page 29), but today they have been replaced by Ryman the stationer and Barclays Bank respectively – and in distinctly uncompromising buildings. The road had been closed to traffic by 1951, and now the approaches are paved with setts.

The Tanner & Chart store in 1904 shortly before it closed for rebuilding: posters in the window advertise reductions on all stock. The street was formerly known as Butchers' Row, and to the right of Tanner & Chart we see two meat traders cheek by jowl. Older Horsham inhabitants remember Messrs Sendall and Fletcher, sometimes a little in their drink, competing furiously for business. Now it is the site of Ryman the Stationer. *Above: John Cannon*

Middle Street with Carfax. Previous views have shown Mr Camplin as owner of this chemist's shop, but in the 1920s it had been successively owned by Gallier and Gooch. Perhaps the incomer was keen to trade on his predecessor's goodwill, since at this stage both names seem to be tussling for attention, with the sign above the door reading 'GOOCH, Late Gallier'. *Above: John Cannon*

Horsham Town Hall. This is a building in two parts. The old market house on the site had been used for the assizes, and when it was converted into a town hall in 1812 space was set aside for courtrooms on each floor. In 1888 it was completely rebuilt except for the north front (seen here) with its arms of the Crown, the Dukes of Norfolk and Horsham. The postcard of 1905 is unusual in that it advertises the temperance hotel founded by Jury Cramp, the owner of a jeweller's shop which moved from Market Square via Middle Street to West Street. The hotel struggled on for about eight years, but virtue was obliged to be its own reward. 'It's an excellent way to lose money,' Mr Cramp would say. *Above: Cecil Cramp*

3

Along the Causeway

The Causeway, *c.* 1906. *John Cannon*

Our walk along the Causeway begins behind the town hall. Little has changed in the thirty years between the taking of these two photographs, but more trees have been planted – as befits a street which has been lined with them for centuries. *Above: John Cannon*

The Causeway from the town hall. The building on the left houses the town's excellent museum, which is a good starting point for any exploration of Horsham. The trees in the postcard of 1903 eventually came to the end of their natural span, and replacements were planted in 1940. *Above: John Cannon*

The Causeway, *c.* 1910. The house in the foreground is a typical Horsham hall house, with two cross-wings, each of which is jettied at the front, that is, it projects above the street. Next to it is a house covered with the ivy which was a popular adornment at the time. *John Cannon*

The two houses have now become one, known as Minstrels, and the removal of the ivy and additions to the façade of the lower part reveals that it was originally a continous jetty house.

The Causeway from the church, with very little change between photographs some forty years apart. A curiosity is the flat gravestone next to the path, which lies north-south rather than having the usual east-west orientation. It marks the resting place of Helena Bennett, who came from the Middle East and who lived at Colgate, a few miles from Horsham, after being deserted by her husband. Her stone has a cross on it, but its positioning satisfied her wish to be buried facing Mecca. *Above: John Cannon*

More continuity in the old house called Flagstones which stands by the entrance to the churchyard. The old postcard was printed in about 1909. A datestone on the central gable claims that the house was built in 1615, but it is being over-modest, Annabelle Hughes, the locally based consultant on historic buildings, believes that the date refers merely to the gable insert and decorative barge-boards, and that the house itself was built in about 1400. The roof is clad in so-called Horsham slabs, the heavy sandstone tiles which are a feature of medieval wealden houses in these parts. *Above: John Cannon*

Garden of remembrance, *c.* 1936. Beyond the church, close to the river, is a small garden given to the town by Councillor Nellie Laughton in memory of her husband and as a First World War memorial. It no longer looks as it did in the photograph above, but it remains a tranquil spot with water running through it. *Above: John Cannon*

River Arun, south of the church, 1938. You need to peer very carefully to make out the church spire through the more abundant vegetation, but otherwise today's scene is very similar to that of 1938. You take the path on the church side of the river to reach the mill on the opposite page. *Above: John Cannon*

Old town mill, 1906. The water was rather deeper in the early twentieth century than it is now, and when Collyer's school was close by the church (page 47) the boys would swim here. The main mill building is now used as offices. *Above: John Cannon*

St Mary's church from Normandy, 1906. The little group behind the street vendor may have been inhabitants of St Mary's Almshouses, the building on the left. The almshouses, founded in 1844, still exist, but they have been greatly altered. A plaque tells us that the west block was rebuilt in 1955 and the east block renovated five years later. *Above: John Cannon*

Collyer's school is today in Hurst Road, off North Street, but it was in this building off Denne Road from 1840 until 1892. Once the boys had gone, Denne Road Girl's School moved in, staying here until it was demolished in the 1960s. *John Cannon*

Sic transit gloria. This playground, with St Mary's primary school behind, is the site of the former Collyer's school.

Denne Road and railway bridge, *c.* 1909. Only a short way from the town centre and these children were virtually in the countryside. *John Cannon*

Today there are pavements and a better surface for traffic, but this remains a quiet spot – and the contours of the road are unchanged.

4

West Street

West Street from Bishopric, 1950s. *John Cannon*

West Street/South Street corner from Middle Street, *c.* 1902. Nos 1 and 2 West Street belonged to Hunt Brothers, silk mercers and general drapers. This was the town's major shopping parade. *John Cannon*

The same spot in 1912 after major rebuilding. Hunt Brothers have relinquished their coveted corner site to the Capital & Counties Bank, but they are still busy trading from no. 2 next door. *John Cannon*

A wider view of West Street from the same position as the pictures on the opposite page. This photograph was taken in about 1929, with Timothy White's sign prominent on the north side, where a long overhang of blinds protects shoppers from the glare. The traffic system is evidently one-way by now, since all the cars and neatly parked bicycles are facing east towards Middle Street. *John Cannon*

There is still a bank on the South Street corner (now Lloyds TSB), with Hammicks bookshop facing it. The buildings on the south side show least change over the years.

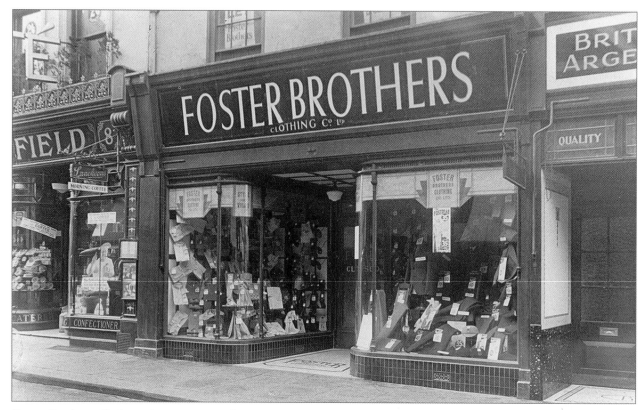

Foster Brothers Clothing Co., *c.* 1925, takes centre stage, with Wakefield's cake shop next door at no. 8. Today the premises are occupied by Birthdays and a Clarks shoe shop respectively. *Above: John Cannon*

International Stores, once a part of any self-respecting shopping street, *c.* 1908. The shop stood immediately to the right of the present cut-through to Black Horse Way. *John Cannon*

Today The Officer's Club sells clothes on the site, but there's a reminder of earlier times in the passage to Black Horse Way – a tiled wall from the old International Stores.

Telegrams—"Sayers, Horsham."   Telephone 11 P.O. Horsham.

Agent for Shippam's Celebrated Chichester Sausages,

AND CAMBRIDGE SAUSAGES.

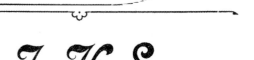

J. H. Sayers,

Fish, Game, and
Poultry Stores.

LONDON HOUSE.

55 West St., Horsham.

Nearly opposite the Capital and Counties Bank,

Agent for Overall Cod Liver Oil.

Comparisons can be odious. Sayers presumably put on an extra special display for their advertising card of about 1912, but phones 4u simply can't compete. The *Horsham Pictorial Trade Record* of August 1912 reports that 'Mr Sayers invariably shows a fine stock of the best classes of fresh water and sea fish according to season, including salmon, lobsters, crabs, oysters etc. The day's supply is on hand by eight o'clock each morning, and the buying at Billingsgate is conducted under the personal supervision of Mr Sayers, whose business also embraces poultry in season, and, as a licensed dealer in game, rabbits, hares, pheasants, pigeons, and partridges and wild fowl are dealt in both wholesale and retail.' *Above: John Cannon*

West Street, looking east. The Horsham historian, William Albery (page 60) was a shy man who hated being photographed, but someone caught him on camera in about 1903: he's in the road opposite the International Stores with a black and white dog close by. *John Cannon*

Some architectural features remain today, but the street is now pedestrianised and the feel of it is completely different.

Looking east from the Swan/Swan Walk, 1885, from a spot just a little further back than that on the previous page. The Swan is on the left, with the Castle Inn beyond it. *John Cannon*

Today one of the entrances to Swan Walk, the large modern shopping precinct, occupies the site of the pub which gave it its name.

The Swan as it was in 1954. *Cecil Cramp*

In today's photograph a mother with her child in a pushchair meets a homeless *Big Issue* seller whose bag and bedding can be seen by the entrance wall.

Woolworths was on the north side of West Street at the Bishopric end. The exterior shot was taken in 1954, but the interior one is somewhat earlier. Everything on display costs either 3*d* or 6*d*, the literature on offer including *Schoolboys' Jolly Book*, *Tom Thumb's Story Book* and *Merry Mites Story Book*. Cecil Cramp

The S. Price printing and bookbinding business stood beween Woolworths and Albery's saddlery (page 60), closing in 1954 after about 100 years of trading in West Street. *John Cannon*

This is the site of the two businesses today, completely redeveloped.

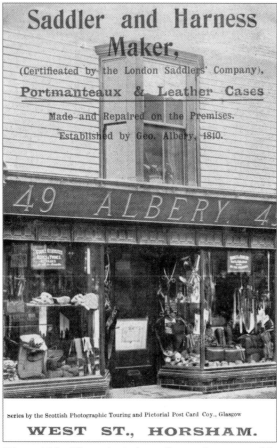

We met Mr Albery just along the road on page 55. This was his saddler's shop in West Street early in the twentieth century. *John Cannon*

Today a branch of the family-run jewellery chain, T.H. Baker, keeps the building in very good heart. Mr Albery generally shunned the camera, but two Baker employees stand proudly outside as in shop photographs of yore. William Knight PJ Dip., the manager, is on the left, with sales assistant David Hodges.

A side window of the premises, along with some of William Albery's equipment, is displayed in Horsham Museum.

Dixeys, West Street. This is the south side of the street, near Bishopric, in 1951 and today. Some of the buildings remain, but Dixeys the opticians seems to be the only constant in trading terms. The Black Horse (next page), known fondly to locals as 'the old kicker', stands on the far corner in the earlier picture but disappeared in 1964. *Above: Cecil Cramp*

West Street from Bishopric. Yesterday's picture, another 1951 view, shows the Black Horse hotel on the far corner, but this has been replaced by an unimaginative block. The scene is utterly transformed. The building on the other corner of West Street is now a vast, brutal edifice (we shall meet it again on page 115), while the Gilbert Rice building has become a McDonald's restaurant. Today's picture was taken from the new Bishopric Square with its Shelley fountain. *Above: John Cannon*

5

Bishopric

Market day at the Bishopric, *c.* 1908. The road was sufficiently wide to allow cattle pens to be erected on both sides. *John Cannon*

The Bishopric, looking east, *c.* 1955. Henry Burstow, the shoemaker and bell-ringer whose *Reminiscences of Horsham* describes life in the town during the Victorian era, was born in one of the cottages beyond the King's Arms in 1828. *John Cannon*

A view in the opposite direction today, showing the modern buildings which have replaced the cottages Burstow knew.

Gone for ever. The houses being demolished in the top picture were 12–14 Bishopric. The council pulled them down in 1931 to make way for the town's very first car park, built (with porticoed lavatories) immediately to the west of the Green Dragon public house, which is seen on the right. The roof of the Congregational chapel in Springfield Road can be glimpsed on the left of the photograph. There seemed little point in including a 'today' picture: the car park site is now covered by the tarmac of Albion Way. *Above: Alan Partridge, below: Cecil Cramp*

Horsham market, looking east, *c.* 1912. The Bishopric was the site of the town's weekly cattle market until 1913, when it moved to the goods yard at the railway station. The house we saw being demolished on page 65 can be seen at the left of the picture, with the Green Dragon just beyond the trees. *John Cannon*

A similar view taken in the late 1940s, with West Street in the distance. This end of the street is now Bishopric Square. *Cecil Cramp*

A very quiet Bishopric, looking west. The postcard, sent in 1915, is entitled 'The old market', suggesting that it was produced after the market had closed in 1913. *John Cannon*

Bishopric Square, with lunching students and precarious skateboarder. The viewpoint is similar, but the two chimneys provide the only evidence of earlier times: the one immediately to the left of the Shelley fountain belongs to the Green Dragon. The fountain commemorates the famous poet Percy Bysshe Shelley, whose family came from the Horsham area, although he was himself disowned by his father because of his atheistic and revolutionary views.

Corner of Bishopric with Springfield Road, *c.* 1907. This imposing building, built in 1899 on land owned by the Roman Catholic church, was occupied by Seagrave's bakery. The delicious smell of new-baked bread rising from the cellars remains a fond memory for many long-standing Horsham residents. *Cecil Cramp*

These same locals know the area as Black Horse Corner, because of the former pub (page 62) on the West Street corner, but in the early fifteenth century the crossroads was known as Lynd Cross – and that's the name given to the modern pub which now stands where Seagrave's was.

6

North Street

Paperboys ready for the off near the railway station during the 1920s. Fifth from the left, wearing a bowler hat, is the man in charge – Queen Street newsagent Mr Duffield. *John Cannon*

Three views of the railway station – *c.* 1906, 1951 and today. The very first station was built in 1848, but the earliest seen here was a replacement of 1859, when horse-drawn buses ran to and from the King's Head Hotel in Carfax. The present building dates from 1938. *Above and middle: John Cannon*

Olive Penfold was a porter at Horsham Station in 1914 when railwaymen volunteered to fight in the First World War. In Miss Penfold's time the service was run by the London, Brighton and South Coast Railway. This became part of the Southern Railway in 1923 and was later swallowed up by nationalisation as part of British Rail. *John Cannon*

Geoff Denman, a member of the railway-platform staff, displays his whistle and train dispatch baton – a recent innovation at Horsham – used to signal to the conductor that it is safe for the train to depart. The railways were denationalised by the Thatcher government, and services through Horsham are now run by Govia.

Station Hotel, North Street. Car hire was one of the services offered by the hotel back in 1910 when the top photograph was taken. Today it's simply called The Station and is part of the countrywide Beefeater chain of restaurants and pubs. The telephone number in the meantime has changed from 'Horsham 16' to eleven digits. *Above: John Cannon*

Newsagents, North Street, 1954. The series of pitched roofs indicates that this business next to the railway station had been expanding steadily. Among the newspapers and magazines advertised here are several that are no longer published, including the *Daily Sketch*, the *Evening News*, *John Bull* and *Picture Post*. *Cecil Cramp*

Newspapers are sold inside station forecourts these days. This grim building stands on the site today, home to a glass firm and a curry house.

North Street, *c.* 1912. Until the market was moved from Bishopric to the station goods yard, cattle and other animals had to be driven between the station and Bishopric every Wednesday. The former double-fronted station building (page 70) can be seen in the distance. *John Cannon*

The bend of the pavement is unchanged, but these pedestrians would be more than a little startled to be confronted by a herd of cows today. The entrance to Horsham Park is off to the left.

North Chapel. So drastic have been the changes to North Street, that it's surprising to find this handsome survivor near the station on the east side. The building dates from the mid-fifteenth century but later additions and changes have been made. It now serves as offices for the PMMS consultancy group. Across the road, near the entrance to Horsham Park, is a cluster of other old buildings which the developers have spared. *Above: John Cannon*

There are no clues along the modernised east side of North Street to the buildings which existed there before. The top picture shows Perry Place, a magnificent medieval hall house with cross-wings which stood on a site south of the ABC (formerly the Ritz) cinema near the junction with Park Street. The house was dismantled in 1912 and moved to Mannings Heath. The building opposite ('Registry office free to servants') has gone, too: it stands roughly on the site of the buildings seen on page 78. Below is an open field years later – just ripe for development! *Above: John Cannon*

Caffyns is up for sale, so this is in about 1980. The ABC cinema is next door. *John Cannon*

The view today. Horsham Arts Centre has replaced the ABC, which gives us our bearings. Caffyns lay to the left of the picture, with Perry Place to the right.

Demolition of old cottages, North Street, *c.* 1950. We're on the west side of the street, and these buildings are coming down to make way for a new public library. *John Cannon*

Today the library itself has gone. This well-proportioned block was built on the site in 1992.

North Street, *c.* 1903. Perry Place is on the left, with Park Street beyond, in a scene littered with advertising signs. We shall get a closer look at the corner building on the following page. *John Cannon*

Traffic signs now predominate in this busy part of town. The old houses on the right have managed to survive the mass rebuilding, one of them the Black Jug pub.

Chart's Corn Stores, *c.* 1910. Amos Chart poses in the doorway of his shop, which stood where North Street meets Park Street and gave the spot the popular name – Chart's Corner. People knew him as Father Chart. *John Cannon*

Today's view changes the
angle: the door on the
extreme left is the one with a
little porch on the older
photograph. North Street
now stops here.

These two views, both taken early in the twentieth century, show opposite sides of the southern end of North Street, which was wiped out by modern redevelopment. Where there was once a raised pavement, now the whole of this section is raised above the gulf of Albion Way. *Above: John Cannon*

North Street looking south from Chart Corner, *c.* 1949. *John Cannon*

This is where North Street now ends and becomes the pedestrianised Chart Way between the Royal & Sun Alliance buildings and over Albion Way. Park Street, which was once a quiet, mainly residential, street now carries North Street traffic south to Park Way – an extension of Albion Way.

Park Street, *c.* 1913. The board on the right encourages passers-by to try this butcher's ox beef and special veal 'if you want to enjoy your Easter dinner'. The shop was situated near the corner with East Street. *John Cannon*

Whereas North Street comes to an end at Chart's Corner, a vestige of Park Street survives some way south of its junction with Park Way. This section has been renamed Park Place and contains just a handful of shops – including Baldock's where the butcher's previously stood.

7
East Street

Stanford's at 49 East Street, 1940s. *John Cannon*

We met the King's Head in Carfax (page 27), and here we see it on the corner of East Street, looking east from Middle Street. The opposite corner is occupied by the shoe chain Freeman Hardy Willis in the 1920s photograph, the manager standing proudly in his doorway with his footwear hanging all about him. Shoes were still sold here in the 1950s, but today the site is an estate agent's. Architecturally this end of the street is little changed. *Above: John Cannon*

East Street looking east, 1904. This photograph was taken a little further east than the previous one. The Anchor Hotel sign can be seen beyond the millinery shop on the right, with another for Horsham Working Men's Club. Another of the town's elaborate lamp standards graces the street further along. Quite a crowd has gathered for the photographer. *John Cannon*

Among the numerable changes in nearly 100 years is the cupola above the corner building on the left of the picture. Shop blinds are no longer in fashion, but the sweet shop Town and Country Weigh still sports one. This photograph was taken from Anchor Court, a passageway which at least remembers the former Anchor Inn on the spot.

East Street looking west, with the Middle Street/Market Square corner at the far end. In the 1910 photograph the benefits of electricity over gas ('large floor space and heavy cost of running') are advertised at first-floor level above Sendall the decorators, flanked by stars studded with light bulbs. Electricity had arrived in the town in 1901. Beyond this building is the Anchor Hotel and its 'motor garage'. *Above: John Cannon*

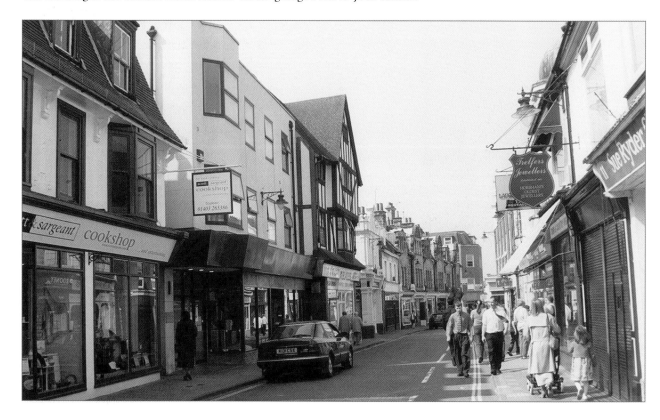

East Street, looking west from Denne Road, 1906. The photographer has persuaded a veritable crowd to pose for him in a beautifully composed picture. The little girl at the front is on an errand with her milk churn. *John Cannon*

The street remains two-way today, but only cyclists may travel eastwards. The buildings close to the camera on both sides of the 1906 photograph are still here, although their uses have, of course, changed. We shall meet the one on the right again over the page.

The location of this building is not obvious, but we passed it on the previous page and now here it is again in 1850 guise: 'A bit of old Horsham' the postcard calls it. In those days it had a fascia of chequerboard brick (apart from the weatherboarded projection at the far end) under a roof of Horsham slabs. *Cecil Cramp*

Today it's the Hong Kong Express and the adjacent part of Pizza Express. In her book *Horsham Houses* Annabelle Hughes records that this was a medieval hall house, and the projecting part was a jettied cross-wing with an upstairs window in the western end which looked up to Middle Street.

East Street/Denne Road. Eighty years on from the splendid 1922 photograph and a newsagent still occupies the corner site. The early picture shows one of Horsham's magnificent lamp standards in the foreground. *Above: John Cannon*

East Street, looking west, 1908. This view is taken from the other side of the Denne Road junction seen on the opposite page. A newsagent was still to arrive on the corner, the premises being occupied by the Beehive pub, run by King & Sons (not yet King & Barnes). Another pub, the Horse and Groom, stands on the far corner, as it does today. To the right, on the corner with Park Street – now Park Place (page 84) – are the showrooms and workshops of F. Brown & Co., cycle and motor engineers. *John Cannon*

The street is busier today, with signs all over the place. The corner shop now sells televisions and similar equipment. In *Bygone Horsham* Anthony Windrum and Annabelle Hughes speculate that this spot may have been the site of the original Saxon settlement.

During the Second World War a huge air-raid shelter stretched along East Street between Park Street and Bartellot Road; it is shown being dismantled in about 1949. Locals enjoyed warming themselves in the aromatic heat rising from the ovens in the cellar of Venner's bakery. *Cecil Cramp*

Today it is the site of the Automate motor parts shop.

East Street. The photograph of about 1900 was taken from a point a little further east than the one on page 93. Venner's bakery (their wheeled carriage and horse and cart can be seen outside) advertised themselves as trading 'under the spreading chestnut tree'. The tree had gone by the time the large photograph on the previous page was taken – perhaps to make way for the air raid shelter. *Above: John Cannon*

East Street, *c.* 1900. We're now reaching the eastern end of the street, with the railway bridge in the distance. The two men on the far left are standing at the entrance to Bartellot Road. *John Cannon*

A wide and busy new road, Park Way, an extension of the Albion Way inner bypass, has appeared on the left of the picture.

East Street/Bartellot Road. In the earlier picture it is 1951 and the site long occupied by C. Brewer & Sons has been cleared for redevelopment. The advertisers have been quick to take advantage, tempting the passer-by with Ovaltine, Bourn-vita, Oxo, Sanatogen Tonic Wine and a visit to the *Daily Mail*-sponsored Ideal Home Exhibition. The ghastly building eventually erected here is at present occupied by Pets at Home, grooming salon and all. *Above: John Cannon*

8

Queen Street & Brighton Road

A parade of the Horsham Foresters past the Queen's Head in 1881. *John Cannon*

Queen Street, *c.* 1906. Queen Street is the continuation of East Street on the other side of the iron bridge which we saw on page 97; this is a view looking west. *John Cannon*

Since lamp standards of an earlier age have been praised elsewhere, it's only fair to draw attention to the elegant modern example on the left of the picture. The new block next to it deserves a much swifter glance and the road is now almost perpetually busy. For connoisseurs 'this is bridge 358 TBHI between Horsham and Christ's Hospital'.

The Queen's Head, *c.* 1912, when the hotel was rebuilt. The board on the right reads 'good stabling', and another on the post of the pub sign 'cycles stored'. *John Cannon*

The pub is virtually unchanged today.

Queen Street, looking east. The earlier photograph was taken in about 1923, when the road surface was sufficiently uneven to allow a cyclist to find a parking place well away from the pavement. There has been little change to the roofline tody on the north side of the street. *Above: John Cannon*

East Street, looking east. The post office previously shared the baker's premises on the left, as a sign at first-floor level in the 1951 photograph still declares; it's now on the other side of the road. East Street ends at New Street, on the left, to become Brighton Road. The Baptist church dominates the skyline in the middle distance. *Above: John Cannon*

New Street. There have been many changes here over the years. The older picture dates from 1959, when the Gardeners Arms stood just a little up the road from East Street. Both sides of the road have been rebuilt in recent years, but the pub sign has been retained (or replicated) to mark the Gardeners Court development. *Above: Cecil Cramp*

Nos 99–103 New Street, 1935. During the 1930s many of Horsham's older buildings were pulled down under the regulations of the 1930 Health Act, and these included a number at the top of New Street. *Alan Partridge*

The site of the cleared houses today, with not a clue to their previous existence.

Upper New Street. This postcard, with its group of happy children, was published in about 1913 by Greenfields shop shown on the near left. *John Cannon*

Today's view is much the same, except Greenfields shop is no longer. Now any shop would have difficulty thriving so far from the centre of town.

Brighton Road, looking towards the town centre with Bedford Road on the right. In the early twentieth century this was known as East Parade; it became Brighton Road in 1906. *John Cannon*

The gateway on the left of today's picture leads to the Unigate Dairy plant.

Moon's Lane, off Brighton Road. The man resting on his hoe in the garden of Moon's Cottage in the 1930s picture was known, one hopes affectionately, as 'Fatty' Parker. These houses were soon to be pulled down. *Alan Partridge*

The old path remains, but the back gardens of Clarence Road now cover the remains of the houses lived in by Mr Parker and his neighbours.

The forecourt of a garage on the corner of Brighton Road and Kennedy Road in the 1930s. Older motorists will remember the days when it was advisable to add anti-knock compound to petrol every other fill. *Cecil Cramp*

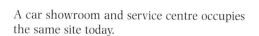

A car showroom and service centre occupies the same site today.

9

Springfield Road & London Road

London Road, *c.* 1900. Wickersham Road, off to the right beyond the brick wall, has now been swallowed by Albion Way. *Cecil Cramp*

Springfield Road, *c.* 1910. This is a view – looking north a little way from Bishopric Square – which has completely disappeared. *John Cannon*

Albion Way now cuts through the former Albion Terrace (on the right) and the Catholic primary school (on the left, behind the railings). The photographs on the next few pages may help you find your bearings.

Springfield Road, *c.* 1910, at the junction with Bishopric, with Seagrave's Bakery (page 68) on the corner. There are two churches on the right: the Roman Catholic and, further away, the Congregational. Posters on the wall between them advertise the Gem cinema (page 116). *John Cannon*

Albion Road, 1951. This was one of the streets off Springfield Road which disappeared under modern developments.

Springfield Road, 1951. A picture taken from the same spot as the one opposite, but a generation or so later. The bakery has now become a hardware store, while the Roman Catholic church has moved (to a site a little up the road on the other side), the building converted for an upholsterer's business. Beyond the Congregational church is the forecourt of the Rice Bros garage. *John Cannon*

All change once again, with the Lynd Cross on the corner, a massive new block on the right of the picture and a new development in the distance.

Springfield Road at the junction with Albion Road, 1954. We are looking back towards the centre now, with the converted Roman Catholic church on the right of the picture and the Rice Bros garage in the centre. Horsham's first cinema, the Gem, opened in the large barn on the left in about 1908. The screen was in the centre, with the projector on one side and the audience on the other, and it had to be regularly sprayed with water in order to maintain its transparency. Albion Road, as we have noted, has disappeared. The Congregational church stood to the left of the photographer, behind the brick wall. *John Cannon*

A view taken from a little further back than the one above. The United Reformed church in the foreground has replaced the Congregational church, while the building behind it stands where the garage and the old Roman Catholic church once were. An utter transformation.

Nos 35–7 Springfield Road, 1933. These houses, north beyond Albion Way, were about to be demolished under the Health Act. *Alan Partridge*

Here's the replacement block today. The Hammonds bedroom store, curiously enough, was preceded here by Hammonds the butchers.

Potter's Corner. This is where Springfield Road, off to the right, meets London Road. In the 1950s view there is a garage a little way along London Road, under an Austin Cars sign. *Cecil Cramp*

Today the corner site is home to a strange-looking building, with flats above a video shop. On the right is a new housing development which follows a growing trend: tall iron gates with entry phones to give a sense of security.

London Road. Just as North Street now stops at Park Street, with Chart Way ushering pedestrians into the town centre, so London Road comes to an abrupt halt at Albion Way, an underpass leading to the pedestrianised Medwin Walk. At the top is the street looking north with the Methodist church in the background. *John Cannon*

The church is still there today, but the new road and a single large building have replaced everything in the foreground of the earlier picture.

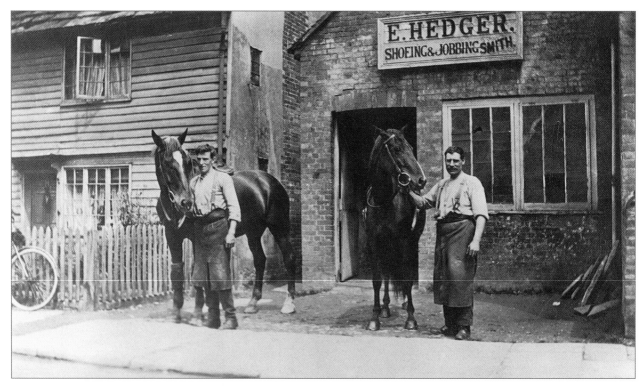

London Road. Hedger's smithy survived on the north side of the street until the 1930s. *John Cannon*

Surprisingly, perhaps, some of the old cottages remain here, but a new development has erased all traces of the smithy.

Those views of London Road (the earlier dating from about 1905) are taken from what is now the end of the road close to the present Albion Way. Wickersham Road once ran off here to the right. In the background to the left Sussex Place adds a Regency touch to this part of Horsham. Until 1779 the House of Correction stood in the vicinity. *Above: John Cannon*

North Parade. In 1903 pedestrians were given more space than traffic on this route out of town from North Street towards Dorking. *John Cannon*

The pendulum has swung today, but it remains an attractive, tree-lined road.

10
Worthing Road

Worthing Road, *c. 1890. John Cannon*

Free Christian church, *c.* 1910. Built in 1721 as the General Baptist chapel, what is now the Unitarian church has played a significant role in the town's cultural history. The Caffyns, Dendys and Eversheds were among the influential local families who founded it, while one of its Victorian ministers, the Revd. J.J. Marten, was instrumental in setting up the Horsham Museum Society. The Friends' meeting house lies close by. *Above: John Cannon*

Worthing Road, looking north towards the centre. Some fifty years separate these two photographs. In the earlier one a road sign directs drivers to the major routes out of town, whereas today this is something of a motoring backwater. Many chimneys have disappeared, but the buildings in the centre have proved hardy survivors. *Above: John Cannon*

Worthing Road, looking south, in the opposite direction from the photographs on the previous page. *John Cannon*

Today the road leads to a busy roundabout, where it meets Albion Way.

Prewett's flour mills, Worthing Road. When this picture was taken in 1951 this mill was producing well over 1,000 tons of stone-ground flour a year, while the family bakery in West Street was turning out some 7,600 loaves a week. *John Cannon*

It closed in 1978, a few years after being bought by Allinsons, and is now part of the Allied Domecq offices. William Prewett not only ran both this enterprise and the town mill close by (page 45), but was involved in a family dairy and an engineering works.

ACKNOWLEDGEMENTS

In a suspicious world the trust and kindness of postcard and photograph collectors shines like a beacon. Two in particular must be mentioned here, both moved by a love of Horsham and a remarkable spirit of generosity to lend me wonderful material for this book. John Cannon has provided the bulk of the illustrations, and I can only hope that he feels I have done them something like justice. Cecil Cramp, well known to local people for talks based on his own prodigious collection, has weighed in with many more and has entertained me with vivid, often humorous, memories of bygone Horsham for good measure. Where I am in error it will be despite their plentiful advice and information.

I would also like to offer warm thanks to Alan Partridge, who entrusted me with invaluable slum-clearance photographs taken by his father in the 1930s, and Peter Trevaskis, secretary of Aldershot & District Bus Interest Group, whose members possess many more photographs of handsome vehicles in a Horsham setting than I was able to use.

Readers eager to discover more will find many interesting books in the library and local bookshops. Authors to look out for include Annabelle Hughes, Anthony Windrum and the prolific Tony Wales, while in 2001 Horsham Museum Society and Horsham Photographic Society jointly published the excellent *Horsham Then & Now*.